OPEN WINTER

OPEN WINTER

Rae Gouirand

Rae Gouirand

for Lucy — with so much gratitude for your reading + friendship through the mysterious michigan web — here's to great poetry coming up through the cracks! XO Rae

Bellday Books, Inc.
Durham, North Carolina & Pittsburgh, Pennsylvania

Published by Bellday Books, Inc., P.O. Box 3687, Pittsburgh, PA 15230;
www.belldaybooks.com

Cover and interior design by Cassandra Patten.

Library of Congress Cataloguing-in-Publication Data

Gouirand, Rae 1977-
      Open Winter: poems / Rae Gouirand.
          p. cm.

      ISBN 978-0-9793376-4-2

1. Americans-Poetry. I. Title.
Library of Congress Control Number 2011933883

Many thanks to the editors of the following publications, who first published these poems:

American Poetry Review:	January
Barrow Street:	Allegory of Good Government
Bateau:	Ask Both; Caveat; Finger; Glass Beach; Ice Plant; Loose; Paper Snow; Translation
Bellingham Review:	Above France; Infinitesimal; One by One; Open Winter; The Rape of Chloris in Two Octaves
Beloit Poetry Journal:	Ufficiali di Notte
Boston Review:	Follow; In Wind: Blunt: Closer
The Canary:	Equals Sign
Columbia: A Journal of Literature & Art:	Forth
Columbia Poetry Review:	Imprimatur
The Concher:	Present Tense
DIAGRAM:	Chordae Tendonae; Sfumato; Solstice
Enizagam:	Moon Jellies
EPOCH:	Foster
Forklift, Ohio:	Plurals; The Whole
Fourteen Hills:	Firewood
Hotel Amerika:	In the Barnes Galleries
The Journal:	Excuses; Lip Reading
jubilat:	By Infinity; Ten Second Windows
The Kenyon Review/KROnline:	Caesurae; Hearsay; Susurrus
LIT:	Visual Interest
LSA Magazine:	Adequate Dissemblance
MAKE: A Chicago Literary Magazine:	Address to Naos
Michigan Quarterly Review:	Ritual Sum; Vanishing Point, 1425
Phoebe:	Ash; The Sands
PMS poemmemoirstory:	Low Stars
Provincetown Arts:	Mira
Seneca Review:	You Form
Slice:	Page of Water; Starwheel
Smartish Pace:	To Scale
Spinning Jenny:	Night in Breath Marks; Passage; Sotto Voce
Tarpaulin Sky:	Sky Page
Water-Stone Review:	Lemon; Night in Winter

"To Emily" appeared in *Visions of Joanna Newsom* (Roan Press, 2010). "January" appeared in *Best New Poets 2009* (University of Virginia Press, 2009). "Ice Plant" appeared in *Best New Poets 2011* (University of Virginia Press, 2011) as well as on *Verse Daily* (June 18, 2010) and *Verse Daily's* Best of 2010 list.

Portions of this manuscript (in earlier incarnations) won the Avery Jules Hopwood Award, the Helen S. and John Wagner Prize, and the Meijer Fellowship. I remain indebted to Dave Smith, Maxine Kumin, and most especially to Richard Howard. For these awards and other gifts of time and support, I thank Bryn Mawr College, the University of Michigan, the Dorothy Sargent Rosenberg Foundation, the Vermont Studio Center, and the Santa Fe Art Institute.

Thanks to Margaret Holley, A.V. Christie, Mark Doty, Mark Wunderlich, Claudia Rankine, Thylias Moss, Stephen Dunn, Alice Fulton, and Timothy Liu for their mentorings while this thing was coming to be. Kim Addonizio and D.A. Powell for the *Best New Poets* nods. Darcie Dennigan, Sarah Wolfson, Ryan Flaherty, Katie Umans: I am so blessed to have you as readers and dear friends. Brent Armendinger I swear. All those teachers, friends, fellow artists, & chosen family whose names are my thousand words for love.

Elaine Equi and Bellday.

My students, who have taught me who I am.

"Address to Naos" is for Brent. "Hearsay" is for Bojana Anglin. "Verjuice" is for Eric Morgan.

I. if the line –

II. even song

III. theme & stain

IV. open: always:

for Ema

(   )

& Rachel

I. if the line –

By Infinity

If the horizon – if the line –
pulls at the eye – pulls a thread

between presence and absence –
is a suture – is a particular resistance –

makes a net of thought – names
a before and after – pulls harder

at what's closed – until there is
a way to leave this – to enter

the coast – to dim the mirror –
to pretend another place for

the wrong bones – for grammar
in stutter – for a dot whose want

to join the line is felt at point –
is every line – is felt in every net –

in every absent trapping – in every
furthest point that reaches every

further point – the verge that holds
its own and knows the distance –

invites the open limit as washing
the face on waking – from brow

to chin – a fold now for the eyes
to close again on the brief shine –

Ten Second Windows

Light as incandescent & loyal.
Loyal as a kind of submission.

Submission as a final saying.
A final line to mark a count.

The line from here thus departs.
Shadow as blame, a fine, a guess.

The line the line. It radiates
its own idea of bareness.

A script. The line here wrong
and final. A business.

Light as incandescent & loyal.
A high dormer over a sleeper.

A far windmill stealing breath
again. Moth from lung, hand

from chest. Song offered to no
address. A pin in wind tracing less.

Present Tense

What minimum: can I
say and say what: is before us:

what is the barest: what is
the middle: the split: of split:

I used to imagine: telling
dreams and: knowing what to tell:

& the need in the telling: like
knowing the ocean made: of lemon

and the single word sweet:
how setting it down and lifting:

it again revealed: the single
thing: one can lift: I ask on & on

water and sleep: and water
can't feel the minimum: so much

as spine: something singing
out complete: and incomplete: out

Forth

Nothing in the world is still:
even at dawn leaves ring in wind

& on & on: each one turning
as an expression: over so much

want: just a wish made &
a sky chilled & an alphabet fast:

time for a long walk. Night
come earlier: shake free a cry

& the chorus we are called:
everything left undone. Watch:

the mess on the breeze circles
something freely: in a light that

glows & wants everything
in it: wants every single swoop

before night spills: loose
& makes heavy: what is mute

Night in Breath Marks

Night is a horse at night. Memory
& empathy a silver

streak between. Sky in the spoon.
Winesap, shadow set.

The child loved marrow & dust
in the light shaft

watching it. The dread of the fact
that it passed

the gold hand. Became time again.
Up the chimney

continuously. No need to draw
the dream is taught.

The square fades & the marrow.
In the seam of the eye

the ever a cover. So much
a shade for the moon

in the way – for the nothing
offered – to close

them & see the only real
we don't.

Mira

Last due date: SEPT 30 1985.
In the margins, some previous reader
pencils in excitement, ringing nouns

with a thin grey line. The circles
gape like heads of nails, breathless
disturbance. Amidst the firmament

the hand connects – graphite scratch
of swift planets, bodies without
address or rest. In later pages,

the halos fade, revealing sharper
points. Arrows fix their objects,
entirely desire. Lucid among the stars,

the bill of a crow indicates
what it wants, pointed, perpetually
hungry capella. This stillness

seems endless. Other stars flicker
in the periphery – chapters pass before
I suspect the descent of Cetus, the Whale,

gloating in a long, complex song,
cool grey recital, every tip gleaming,
x and y axes twisting for radiant

emphasis. A half-erased cross flashes
at his fluke, between mass and muscle.
Periodicity has been underlined twice.

I lean in to the varying star, her red rise
blurred by pages' faces, and darken
dim Mira, the asterisk he uses to push.

Ash

If every evening could give itself over
to ash, letting fall

the morning's pronouncements, letting go
the shapes of words.

Under the faucet you rinse soot
from your hands,

one assuming the other, slipknots
of fallen water.

Ink kindles, heightens, takes
its final place.

Blackened roses soften, then diminish
under touch.

Passage

Wind: hurls leaves at the door: I hear
the color: I think you're coming
singing: mathless: one bound

curve. A morning: the act
of drawing the state of being drawn.
Resistance: a body on a surface that moves.

Shapes change even in a single voice.
Leaves at the door you don't
have to ask for. We pull:

and pull a necessary tract:
anchor the alphabet that needs no
spelling out. To anchor the change.

For the lapse in time. For the area
large or small: definite or not.
Put beyond doubt what

asks nothing. Asking:
implies no more than the putting
of a question. Ask: implies no more than

the statement of desire. Does it depart
the passage or set an emblem
in it. Does it stretch from

the inside: get the body
involved. Take a changing
shape. Mark me I: ask blinking.

Measure the meaning. To blink in wind:
a glyph: a fact. In doorways: voices
carve. No falling mark.

Low Stars

The sea drags, the moon drags. It's not
your turn. We're drifting to sleep

in a noiseless cove and no one knows us.
No light comes in. Worth knowing

how time passes through this, how we keep
the sweeping with seaweed & faint cloud,

measure our particular instance.
In climbing, no ache is a surprise, no *please*.

Shadows make figure eights in my blood,
blood drifting, sleep drifting,

sounds drifting like a cloud over my lap,
schemes dissolving to brighten

the points of low stars. Forced and nestled
they may be right, they show only

in the weave through which I feel self
twisting. Not my turn, not

tonight. If I want to climb I'll
do it alone, the moon pulling behind,

hunting, holding. On nights
with no moon the coast known by heart.

Stars turn with eyes and in eyes.
That simple fact like that of the bird —

I watch, it flies. A spine. Its stretch
presents me, vertical or curved, points

my silent seal. Or lays me out by the fact
of lying down, the return the *please*

the fish gleaming in the shape of sleep,
carrying their drift in the skin

of drifting. The sounds that lack
in your ears are the sounds of cotton threads

discussing their place with the moon.
The voice you hear first discussing something.

You Form

Before sex she is warming each finger in my navel
while telling me about an old myth of formation –
that oysters rise to the surface of the sea one hour each night
to inaugurate their pearls. There they unhinge to capture

drops of rain or dew before returning to the sea-bed, where
waters transform in years of darkness. Behind my lids
I see the flickering hyperbole of these creatures' prize dreams
like light splattered on their inner walls, their twitching

musculature burying the point of contact, effusing stunned
lumps of cold gunmetal, inky blue, orange in Burma,
golden in the Philippines, silver and rose off the Australian
coast, the mornings flushed with those beginnings.

The women in our families all married in pearls, their
rolling voices at the collarbone in ceremony. My neck
still knows their exact weight, that sweet sixteen strand.
They came in a box that snapped when it opened, with a note

in ink on ivory. More unblinking and lunar than our eyes,
the loop rests by the mirror – mothers and aunts and sisters
staring back from the constant round. Spheres that loosened
in the mollusk's soft tissues, without points of fixation

to mess a symmetry. No mark of fierce attachment, buried
molecule, gaping mouth to the interior. No nascent clue.
Pearls which contain no central nucleus, no sandy grain
or slip of wood. A white strand. It seemed best. Our eyes

trace each other, two across a small hard knot, color rising
in the nacre, the crystal thickening. Along my kneecap, ankle,
hipbone her lips suggest the asymmetrical semi-round,
the irregularly shaped droplet, the gorgeously deformed

baroque, the ridged cerclée. Her tongue turns the pearls out
and they press each other insistently, a gothic form coming
just at the hinge of my feeling, as jagged and monstrous
as the emptiness of a ravine. Glowing a coppery brown

with something dark and liquid at its middle, its fogged face
conceals the slick of a fish once fixed in the shell's blue
walls, buried under the ripple of some possibility,
frozen into the face of its only hour of becoming.

High Street

Her pager and lamp in the middle of the night,
questions for police and rustling for forms.

Dishes stacked in the sink, pipes
lurching empty noise. Snow drifts fastened

the windows, thin strips of cold.
The lights' blankened glance.

We fell asleep at night neither asking
nor responding, hoped the snow

would deepen some as we slept through
just once. A salt song paused

around our ears as strangers culled
casually let trash. There were only

a few houses before they moved on,
up the windy alley to the rest of town.

Starwheel

Words and their meanings
speak: of necessity and difference:

guilt the same as thin
feeling: speaking as heartbeat

felt: I tell someone a story
about oblivion and: the meaning

is the return: like witness
to white space: like the isolation of

the moon: what is chased
seems the space between: what

we know and what we want
more of: my friend says gossamer:

I ask: what do you mean
by anything: if the answer comes

it is everything: if it holds
the same it is no less: undoing

Page of Water

If freedom can be found
in prison: if waking is like hearing

the voice: of a room
calling to you from across water:

if the page: calls to
the water and calls: you peer into

the space between
the walls and beat your pulse: if

you try quietly to exist
while light gradually finds a slant

to climb: if it climbs
and thus saves us again from

nothing: if we refuse
answers to the wrong questions:

if I swallow: so swallow
another piece of invisible space

Ask Both

What area is a word if you
ask: for wind you get stones if you

ask: for stones wind: ask both
and stones in wind stones: in wind

wind passes: on its way
to being wind: and walks out the hills

to bend them: it whistles
what is not stone: or wind or fence

the bird: stands midair
a constant line: the stillness of stone

the only thing reminding
of moving I think: back what you said

about cold stones and dirt
holding in your ears and cast: some

tones if you ask: the words
turn so ask: just one word to fold

Finger

Ask once and no response:
can mean no response: ask twice

and the same only points:
like a finger to the moon: silence

indicates: the keeping
of space: as yes it must be known

when unsaid: twice
the telling happens: only when one

is ready: to be alone with
what is told: the work of rope:

a cast a discipline
a letting: I want to desire nothing

more than the state
beyond need: recognize the moon

bow speaking: the word
after the edge after: the felt point

One by One

Who stops to breathe: the moon
smooth as a pillow as

communion: or turns to leave
some silver in a jar atop

the refrigerator: the bank dark &
glinting: who stops to count

how many moments are felt
at once and the mouth:

making each zero: as it grows
who stops to ask what

they'd choose: going on or
not: the moon keeping

every bit we toss up: how far
we are: our nearer stars

wearing thin & these breaths
coming one: by one

In Wind: Blunt: Closer

Leaves sinking freezing: sky
breaking down as restless: I turn

& take: take up the vacant
space: the vacant eye flips up:

this point in November
the point: that leaves sink & wheel

in wind: blunt: closer
to the braid I trace underfoot:

tracing saving it: saving
the night in a pocket: it cannot

pass through the tiny hole
it cannot: take up a second song

I pass through myself: let
evening come: let it take us up

and rename the world: let
it take hold & rename the world

II.   even song

Paper Snow

All that remains: between
the cold and the feeling of cold

is the old glass: sliding
liquid sand blown flat and cut

for this: and taped:
to its inside face the white sheets

of paper snow: folds
and cuts the same on the window

as letters cast: to
readers we can only suppose:

hang paper snow inside
the window to show the window

for what it can be on
days spent: diamonds waiting for

light: there is nothing for
this space: no emptiness to end it

Plurals

What is there to weep for:
there are so many: so many to fold

into folds of one: plus one
plus one: sheeting rains the sheets: make

and make and: make more
to feel: more is not more but still

it moves me: like the moving
through of mouth on mouth: still and

open: the dearest counterfeit
handwritten: I say in your hand when

I mean out: of your hand
into mine to be turned: what we turn

inside: the word before it is
spoken: there is nothing not plural:

not in any one: nothing not
openly counting and mouthing the count

Sky Page

Saint Lucy had her eyes about her.
The eyes of the martyr. The eyes

of the body & the eyes of the world
blinking. Everything I see returns

the eyes. In every fence that marks
a place. Every fence makes a place

in it – in its water, in its stance.
The eyes move over this & take it.

Seen it is changed and made a breathing
thing. A thing with wings held near

a sky page. The eyes of the saint
wait on the body. The eyes of the saint

mark the attempt & the course. I would
take her arms & pin them back

to ask the dark part, the pupil. Eyes
in it sing mine & mine & mine.

Never come back into two points.
Lenses spill and bounce. Water

sinks the eye further. I would look
for water in her. I would start looking

harder. I would look to her at my
return, look up again to near the word.

Visual Interest

Peacocks came up from the neighbor's
and paused in the yard, ankles ringed – zoo gates
ajar down the hill. Every breath against the window

a minute cloud. Mother bathing the baby
upstairs. My singular sight. The birds swim slowly
through my pupils – vast bouquets of green mirrors, scrim

of secrets. The lawn turned by turquoise,
midmorning extends multiples, long and poised
as solitude. Facing the house, they spread their plans

– is there music on their side of the glass? –
compose their upright robes – serrated shine – all in
sequence. No street. Arcs, stairways of broken faces. The aperture

blurs in the waves of blue. You see –
said the feathers, bared like ribs.

Foster

Ashes of roses to aid
the process. Here comes
the lantern man to the station.

Forget & make
room for a coterie of
false beliefs, a thousand times

yes. This simple
silhouette. The notion
held in fists protecting a head.

You've already been
decided. Quiet knot tied in
lost string. Cold nose directed out.

Ufficiali di Notte
Florence, 1432

As twilight hums and men are released from
professions, the Office of the Night knocks,
checking at houses with sons, probing

neighborhoods near the unfinished dome
for nocturnal codes and conjugated
accusations. The great oculus squints

at moving corners of shadows, the edges
of palaces and sheds where the city is undone
by its civics. Your family has dismissed you

from evening meals, and in this particular lane
a cloud of others' suppers wafts from houses
where your presence would invite visits,

fines, beatings, worse. According to neighbors,
who have been asked, you couldn't care less
about sex, never a woman swelling in

your parents' house. Unseeing of your acts,
they sleep through your entrance at some
late hour, edges rubbed ragged with imprints

of architecture, the rough fit of your front
into the urgent curve of that arch where you
let him pin you. Your ribs undone by the press

of the sandstone, you've just glimpsed the math
radiating from the perfect circle, these structural
thrusts. In every alleyway, men slur

the hymn of the half-done dome, a deadened
overture to the brickwork that hollows above
the streets. Another's hands on your waist,

your shirt pocket tears from the weight of
wages' hard round mouths, national faces
stamped on their surfaces. These spill from

the rip down your marble-cold legs, lost in
the cobblestones, the only things you abandon
when those who have heard your mouthings,

the tracery of your breath, come with their lanterns,
set you running through the streets, released
like an integer from flourishes of stone.

Equals Sign

Quinta, five-pointed star,
sign for war, pain, & festivities,
star of haste, I am doubtful —

the lapis galaxy splinters
instinct; mercury slipped in
has unturned our screws.

Rain freezes on the course
of a low voice, multiplies
the cadence of a dangerous

neighborhood. The first bruise
seems ultramarine. Signs for
temporary work & lodging

on the wrong side of a wall.
The arrow of me curves around
a station where blood might prove

a monogram. You gone into that
soprano crux, cold pronunciation.
My thinking about card games

& proofreading, fixed as a ceiling,
the fermata, finally over. The two
angles inside my hands have not

understood, occupy with exponents
of themselves, bones of red cardinals.
Our antenna delivers so many

kinds of rain. The unknown sex
singing among the blood oranges.
How a child reduces the almanac.

Infrared symbolon: we break
this slate between us, take
a piece to mark us in return.

To Scale

(Broken Dishes '19 Grandmother's Garden '32
Apple Basket '55 Ohio Star '69)

These were the grand medallions of your education –
this stitchery's precision, this chintz burial, a ceremony
for summer evenings spent on the porch with women
who do not speak as they tender their lines.

(quercitron, logwood, purples derived from lichens,
cochineal, woad's oldest blue)

Across your four pairs of knees the quilt is rotated
ninety degrees. Husbands, eyes closed in their rocking
chairs, consider only the moral industry of your sex,
your quickness with those sharp wands, the expertise

(quadrant diagonal cells' bisection obtuse angling
unilateral triads whitework flowers)

of your hands with these treasured bags of scraps.
The strange symmetry of your feeling radiates
between your laps, sprawling geographies pieced
from the most intimate of fabrics – the cream satine

(wedding skirt against woolen collar night veil Sunday
draping daughter's first blanket)

of a waistband, the turkey red of an autumn jacket's
pleat, the print of peonies a bonnet that sat behind
your pulse. The precious profuse bouquets on dark
background, a bolt made in Provence – your favorite

(scenics, fancy stripes, woodland, vermiculate,
chinoiserie, urns, haloed geometrics)

dress passes, fluttering in squares, from one pair of hands
to the next, its weave kept under fingers' silence,
sweat clenched in its minuscule print easing needles that
corrode overnight. Untucking pins, your companions

(dimpled challis, velvet blocks with palm-pressed
piles, ribbons' trimmings, pintucks)

baste neighboring pieces, holding down cells with fingertips,
metal pushed through fiber's giving space, pulled out again,
creating a geology, puckers and the raised ridge of intent,
figures affixed into permanence by the thread's catch –

(insides fashioned from babies' bibs, sheets worn thin,
curtains arranged in internal stars)

top, batting, and backing, held in place by a single hard strand,
invisible but for the texture it leaves, the dotting of fingerprints.
As you work, the only audible discussion – regarding the name,
which is based on the top surface alone, its public lines,

(buttonhole stitch square knot slip stitch running
stitch xxxxx)

though on the back, touching your thighs, lay the perforated
trails, the exacted push of nimble decimals, footsteps hushed
in swollen lines under which you will sleep, caressing
the embroidery of a name upon the impressed rules.

(Touching Stars Triple Tulip Red Birds Double
Wedding Rings Unnamed Pattern)

Address to Naos

State without state, clearer than the address
& not kept by it, you are nothing

of your surrounding. Are slant between space
as space between. Patient as nurse

you shed your luck for darkness, never count
within a room for form. Amid

matter you are never one to state the matter
evenly. There is no argument

to be found with a thing that leaves the worry
of stability to the cell and the cell

by its side, moves between them or erases
between them or takes from

between them nothing either measures,
calling none of it *this* or *own*.

Excuses

The keys I forgot by the side of the bed.
That I woke up yesterday feeling.
What I felt. What message
hid in the rest.

Imbalances on the table and in the chart.
On the pyramid of basic need, food
& roof first. An evolutionary
tendency toward

the worst. Scissors in hand, a string
tight round the neck. Hands that
let lots slip. What you thought
without reading my face

for what it really said. Then what
you did not and did. Never once
a decent chance. All amiss.
More coincidence.

Imprimatur

The main body of my work, he says
with his hands in his pockets, *deals with*
very brittle matter, namely, glass. On his grid,
a wisteria divided into nine hundred and sixty-six
precisions plus base, hemisphere broken on a fault

where the curvature splits on the page. The lamps
are made for sale, mostly — this one, a request
by a woman who already owns a couple
in the irregular lower border group,
sees bedside space for a third.

Louis fancies the idea of replacing
the shade's open peak with some more
work, a crown that connects more clearly
the panels to their weighty base, furthering
the effect. He erases the straight edge and tries

a network of pendant branches. *Won't convince*
all subjects, he notes, bent over the science:
sometimes horticulture's a *pain in the ass.*
Though the wisteria clicks, he frowns.
Where the lightbulb would disclose,

invention conceals. How tight
will Edison's lips seal at the sight?
Can he be persuaded by "the dependence
of translucence upon its radical," etc? Will
juries term this turn — "irregular upper *and*

lower border group?" The fuss. Louis massages
the dips in his temples and refocuses his eyes
above the bevy of flickers. Painting wasn't
sharp enough, photography had no room
for signatures, ceramics never offered

the remote comfort of the lamps'
copper strips, soldered and sentimental,
lustrous. Outside, the night deepens behind
the trees, the fields' edges dimming to vibrations.
Impossible to separate hues from the determining light,

every surface a sort of sconce as the globe slips behind
its dark drop. *Am I sexy enough to propound
these superlatives?* He switches off the light,
leans back in the slats of his chair,
and squints out at the lines.

Sotto Voce

Here below, the governed.
A pool of glass with its transparence
and counter, one hand under the other. Thinner

marks of law and prayer.
A lip's uncertain tremor. Leave it
in the distance and turn over. Two give and shift

their order. An even song
could tear her. A twin song belongs
here. For what the tongue might cover. Can you

hear the summer vapor
humming as it hovers – one hand
reaching under the other, into the truer color.

Sfumato

n. the blurring or softening of sharp outlines in painting by subtle and
gradual blending of one tone into another. [Italian, past participle of
sfumare, to evaporate, fade out.]

Inside La Specola, a woman's neck graced
by pearls, comma between face and science.
Entirely wax, aside from that string, as though
a woman sculpted on such a cold table deserves
something for the borrowing. Hair, also real, kept

in braids, some warrant of care or purpose for this
surrogate, a sample years past her one stopped
utterance for Florence, its students of bodies
& service. The city stands, wax intact,
but I learned my veins from books,

guessing faint hairpin turns in blue
x-ray, and a house where things pulsed
without the rise of sight. (A mother, once
chamber, confabulates from a hill address –
pick ascent or decline, but just decide.) Spectacle,

the small lift tab on her chest, sliding our eyes under
her sides: heart, kidneys, liver, uterus purple, high-
ways of veins – of course I'd think highways –
& muscle rivers, system of blood and reason,
of room, beauty, clauses. One thing

granted her above her neighbors:
she moves, or seems to. One leg, flung
ajar, a pubic curtain – tickling, or nerve, or breeze
disrupts what is otherwise the model's solid promise,
more perfect than a brighter face, bleeding out beneath gaze.

Full-bodied modesty. How does wax understand witness,
keep plague in a box, resist? Studies of muscle have
dressed these walls for centuries, & she continues
to look up & show what she has, some colored
organs, held in their shaped chambers, curved

& corresponding. Suppose you would allow
your hands (mine, voice of course) to examine
that fit, in the wax or in the wrist (once broken, still
senses), and find something you actually could not speak
to, that did not arrive from biology's solid case. Moth, memory,

(bed), box. With lock. What might that cavern feel like, in hands
accustomed to one piece atop, askance, aside – constancy
of purpose, determined rules of surface? When I glance
sideways at the distant past, I can kind of feel it, but
the edges elude – no protrusions, & those what

I go back looking for. If my mother says
(what she says) about long ago, she can progress
past the brief dent of the question – but yesterday,
no such luck. A sequel to (fill in stages of abuse) leaves
the sentence in a state of. Encephalopathy: comma's pause & the

rest never comes. When I learned to read maps (interest) she flipped,
as with the horticulture bit. Ontogeny recapitulates phylogeny
he said, ninth grade (won't forget). The art in Italy is so
large I can't make everything out, but am satisfied by
what foregrounds suggest. Each leaf echoes

later mass. Vein law: eventually, it feeds back in.
(Not that I meant. The rest recedes.) A guide: da Vinci
favored that film in the distance, translucent veils overlaid
for atmosphere, estimate of haze. Vague sense of movement
delivered by breath (in) rather than (front page). Something comes

into view if we choose, put one foot in front – but first, its
muted face, fuzzy guess of the thing, perhaps its king
-dom, granted that it lives. Asks for your immediate
pause as it adjusts, fits to your lens, then appears,
one day, harsh defining stroke. Blade lands

noisily in the thick top of a chest. When
you see this chest it stings so bad you can't even
focus. Its boxness could not be worse: solid, kept, and
filled. Contact can be so cruel. Wish you'd never glimpsed
a calligraphy so awful and readable, characters of such brutal

defects, entire vocabularies of soundless tissues and bruises.
Far better to see the skin as more than it is. The woman
in pearls as woman, not willing. Even if she never
took a breath from the room, kept her own, had
only her sterile clarity and arranged hands,

turbinate and permanent, before the constant
flux of us. During the Renaissance, art arrived
from the eye rather than the divine. I was inspired
when they looked up in 1400 and saw parentheses' glint
around the suggestions of things: ought to research popularity

of halos, to know what was thought about such signs. Seems
from what I've seen that everything graduates from single
stark details, nicks in the surface that force us. A cornea,
if scratched, handles its damage in flood; we insist on
patching. My fist went straight for hers when I

was two. Uncut nails, & that the last she saw of
me, I believe. My family insists on duties, such as:
loss (memory, present tense), forgiving (for remains
of time & these lesser horizons), and chronic anything.
The vocabulary of new information & episodes, sunk by

anterograde amnesic difficulties. No wonder the masters
found joy in observation, apprenticed themselves to
anatomists and spent their pens on messages of
the inner life instead of waiting for the next
annunciation. Did I forget to mention one

of the women in question – it won't add much,
I guess. I'd rather examine the symmetry of what's
simplest – fall's coming, preparing the press. Perhaps
it's easiest to say in terms of lease, time and space a grant
greater than land. Those contents refuse to empty their news

unless. Sooner or later the ribcage deflates (see now the heart)
when the subject's given its proper name and admitted to its
components. Acquisitions include apples, aphids, emeralds,
lost cells, all escaping details delivered to distance. Neck
-lace a final trace, what we've required of ourselves.

III.   theme & stain

Open Winter

Light has risen & spread itself thin.
The hour between here & dreaming.

Eyes weave scene with scene.
At every turn growth splits & takes

room from absence. Scars of pith
on aspen twig. Grass guards silence

on its tips, offers frost to space. Mice
sleep in wickless & iced hiding, letting

go the time. White sky flashes & waves.
Lumen accumulation, curtain of blur,

quiet static. An arbor winters songs
of pea-green vine & I knit with steps

the number of times we cross in thought.
Chest parted & breath opened to cold.

Any thing glows & exceeds its given.
Needles drop on the white path,

summons in focus. There is only
so much stillness inside an eye.

The slow iris offers no promise.
Downhill the river rushes past,

cold Ohio water knowing nothing
of ending, only its present name.

Translation

A window is just a piece
of glass in front of a view: and the slight

paneness of the light caught
in it: light caught: the ear erases nearly

everything that catches: imagine
a kiss there and how it moves feeling away

from any line that's being drawn:
how a circle can go in a circle without hurting

to be a circle and can show its own
shape in shaping: can this sense be enough

for you it is: for me that's
the question I realize constantly: imploding

and integrating what a question
always does: what any word can for instance

just: which asks not just what but
what a word like just could ever really mean

Hearsay

My friend explains a tense
in her native tongue reserved: for

hearsay: for what has passed
that you didn't yourself witness but

pass in speaking: we mistake
hands & leaves picking the last

grapes & grapes gone to raisin
under September moon: asking if

there are circumstances when
it's best to keep yourself in: here's

another: these have dried around
their seeds and glow: now fingerprints

on fruit skin: not a far color
from the stains we wake to find but

sticky sweet still: is it better
to be understood or to be loved

Glass Beach

Of the millions each chooses some
to keep: another year's tossoffs

glittering now underfoot, tesserae
that we exclaim & take for

shape, for luck, for what: we don't
know but need odd pieces

for. Sometimes you break glass
exactly, nipping the line

for that sweet crack: almost as
precise as want or hurt: I

watch you choose, and space them
in your palm: blue lacuna blue

& throw the sharp ones back. After
some fizz the pacific is new

again unmoved: blue flows over blue
& breaks & breaks into place

Allegory of Good Government
L'Effetto del Buon Governo, A. Lorenzetti, 1338–40

Pace seems a lettuce in thin celadon,
fat braid under her hand. Sister Fortezza

resists her vision, fist shut on spilled
emotion. Prudenza, did you drop

your tongue once? Your crown lain
on a cobweb veil. Your Latin

all capital & gold thread. You point
rather than speaking your phrase

& neither other stares. Why
should no eyes cross in this court?

Why the free heel turned to crop
us? Only the shrouded guards

who whisper at your knees. With faces
shaped like slaps. We all know the fact

of the corner behind us & our names
constantly over our heads.

The Rape of Chloris in Two Octaves
La Primavera, S. Botticelli, 1485

The thinnest scrim wakes
just before it is lost – beyond
his shoulders appears a blue place,

windy always, dye
of deep water & the sky
that corresponds, and from it

he dives, stretch
of his lack, & under
this force – not *realize* so much

as *release*. Knowing
this, my lips split, & I find
a choke of flowers in my teeth –

thin red things
bursting, worst in high season,
bent backward & glancing at his

blue hand.
The horrible glimmer
of living things. Zephyr sees

something gorgeous
in their glare – this was
the ceremony's theme & stain.

The dress is
endless: poppies shine
their highest agitation, every hour

so open, their color
an octave higher in its reds,
caught in the cloth. I could swear

to their taste
but no longer trust
the tongue – it's lost

all sense
of sentences,
& is supposed

to stay
dumb as the face
examines all times.

Flora I am
called since, & stand
on the face of a clock

that never
turns, calling up violets
from a constant spine of cold.

Adequate Dissemblance

In the earliest scrawl of human pursuit,
scratched on an antler in a rock house

in Auvergne, the naked hunter, approaching
the ample Urus, who is eating a little grass,

pulls his spear back in the air. This clutch
will become the D, the fist of motive.

An R emerges from the predacious rip
of the open mouth. The creature

will vanish, but the antlers, V.
What of this to I the child, left to

the dining room table long past the clearing
of the dishes, the plate of cold eggs

leaking, m n m m n against the edges
of the vegetables and the quiche,

the serum of barely solid foods.

Moon Jellies

In college, in Florida, she followed friends to the beach,
to cloudlessness, to another study of the world:

to the bright towel, to darkening skin, to the way
that salt air increases sweet and fat. What I understand

is the world of water, I told her: what I once wanted
more than anything was my own way to

the blue. I would have given anything to join it,
& have spent my time washed in its reflection.

She tells me a story: even in winter they'd go
& make a game of flinging moon jellies back out

to the waves, seeing who could send the furthest
sail. So close to moonlight, so close to water,

they were both visible and invisible. We are
nothing. Transparent things touch transparence,

and belong to it. I understand. Why is it so important
to kiss someone on the mouth? Sometimes it just is.

Caveat

I have not claimed to claim
anything: beyond a few questions

carried: like old sense in
the wrist that highlights: when it rains

and sings when pinned
in dream: so the sleeping voice turns

nothing: more than sovereign
nothing: no more a ladder by the house

but the wave: to rise on it
debris: to rise on it words: like exes

making faces in the spelling
that so leaves us: vibrating our shapes:

if a woman wants to ask
a question: can we leave it hanging

and let that: be the act
that saves us from again forgetting

Caesurae

The moon is half: an emergency
I am: the madeleine in shadow

invoked but not enveloped: born
with blue eyes my color

redoubled: a guessed-at form with
an opal in her throat. I was

told the scratch would close but
on the cliff of this tongue

opening on knowing: scores rise
to one corona. But were

mountain flowers still inside me
spitting filigree: were these

holes fact and not space between:
a chain of annotations for

spark and finish: the line of salt
a diary: I need no pale word

In the Barnes Galleries

Sunday afternoon in the Barnes galleries,
I'm on the second floor musing
what hidden prescription

Dr. Albert C. Barnes imagined for his
constant collection, ever-nude
women. Though without

any mention in the guides, some series
in ironwork, black antiques,
reflect possibilities

from their locations. Sharp, eclectic,
voicing proximity, shears fix
a Matisse headdress

in place, an ancient protractor points
at doorless hinges, pokers direct
their multiple prongs. Pressed

to believe in coincidence, I'm counting
the keys he hung in this last room,
the walls reserved for favorites –

women far from surroundings. In Renoir's
green fields, the nudes are turned
from our side of this. Six

or so, fair-haired and amazingly pale,
sexless, none turn a gaze
to the brackets

at their edges – demonstrating scroll,
asking interest. Adjacent to this,
Van Gogh – *Nude Woman*

on a Bed. She's wearing forgotten stockings,
more naked than without, as if the time
spent removing them would undo

the want. Respirating, brunette, pubic,
all armpits and legs, hair ordered
by technique, hips against

the white backdrop, defiant navel dark
and small. Hard to tell if the light
suggests the stay of night –

regardless, she's not asking alleviation,
posture freed of plainer notion.
Was his triumph

or trepidation, adding her to the rest,
tacking her between Renoir
and the doorframe?

Next to this, nothing ferrous, no
tiny hook for a white coat.
Her needless gaze

returns no question. This is an empty
consultation. When she pulls
her hands from behind

her head, she will stand, breasts resuming
volume, reach for her robe,
and walk away from us.

Loose

The hinge is delicate the pin:
coming out. The bed

bends: wood under us again
it is too early: to spread

so wide: & vanish like this
but I'm watching: spread

for it: the *like* or *as* that is
the sky we have inside

us slipping: I can't explain
I am holding something:

meaning made in my hand
it is rare. & so loose:

loosen with me again: aloud
we cannot speak of it

so close: I don't want the air
to quote me on this

Follow

What can I put that won't follow
or stick: to the white

we rely on for whiteness, for dawn:
what we must. The sun

to blind us enough, to help us go on.
It's always: in motion

the question burning its mark as
it goes: what are these

words. What is their relationship
to light. What do I even

remember about my life. I open
a book at night: copy a line

again. It copies my tone: dares me
that white on its face

demands: that I write it, that I
too come undone

Firewood

White: quiet on everything
on everything it weighs: the trees

the fence the roof:
the horizon more equal for it.

In the morning all it is
is cleanly ours: it bears no tracks.

It bears the quiet: holds
its crush before the light: the blue

pooled here & there,
the first pale gold coming to

the firewood. Sometimes
it's too late to fall asleep at all:

I ask, read me your favorite
line: will you before the globe

shakes itself awake: we all
need something to hold us down

Lip Reading

Under the lapping fan
the neighbor's threatening tones on
the dogs, the downhill reverb of sleep trains

heading east and the woman
upstairs talking on the phone, walking
from one room to the next and opening a drawer

to take out something she needs.
The rattle of everything inside it resettling.
This number cannot fit in a square so much as

a circle. In my eyelid. The fact
is there are two of our kind. The walls
are disguise. I will finish telling you tomorrow.

IV.   open: always:

The Whole

Pupils attend their teachers: but we
can only see one: at a time unable to split

our own line of sight in two:
enlarging & darkening like any real

thing like any pool: that is large
& black & drinking: take and take to

absorb: the pupils always black:
all absorbing: if you look at the point

where you would reflect in another's
eye: you see what you have become there:

what has become: what mixing of
color and dark pressed into felt: the pool

through which we move or don't
and don't but only become: what we see

in being seen: the whole in the whole
in the middle: of the point elapsing silently

Chordae Tendonae

To draw a line bone to bone
along the front of the throat: move

the name from its closed
word to confuse: sympathy and

confusion touch me: like
this to confuse the sense but not

the feeling: to sympathize
my piece of skin with its undersong:

say *heartstrings* and list as
you graze them: they keep the door

in place: move your hand across
the sacrum: cup an unspelled word

between touch and telling
fingers trace the strings: sympathize

their job: that tender pass
aches between water and its shape

Solstice

I have a friend who capitalizes
Always: why must I on

silent days describe how it feels
to breathe: how the last day

feels before it breaks in the cold
for all the slowly breaking

cold: the piece we keep on such
a day: on the hinge of all

changing days someone else's
fire: far away I want

to know the why for why I reach:
why do I hold my breath

& hold so much: & listen for
the catch: not because

the glowing holds but by that
light we kneel: & know

Ritual Sum

—— Tonight I crack the window and pull back the sheet
to remember our neighborhood in Michigan. In summer,
up cobblestone for an egg cream, peeling old paint

on the deli porch as dusk sank between houses of brick.
Then threading home down the quieter streets, tracing
the living room lamplights of those who had settled

their things past & their August plans. At the last house
before our turn, the trumpet flowers – a side yard steeped
in the sturdy perfume of ghost bells that sliced the air

with their liquor at night. I'd stop there every time,
and remember what their master said one evening –
that their scent caused narcosis for those

who inhaled deeply, or nightmares for sleepers
in their shadows. He shared the Latin names from
his chair there under the radio, a tinny box pointed out

the kitchen window. In dead of winter, that radio fuzzed
to ice as I continued to walk past, hands knotted inside
pockets, thinking of what lay waiting under the snow.

Even gone they caught my breath. The chairs empty
every evening heard what I wanted to add, offered surface
to long gaze. I'll linger there tonight with eyes closed.

Lemon

The notion, the wholeness, glows in fog,
its own envelope. The first firm one

scenting the tree, lucid in juice, thick with
cold pigment, rich in heady oil, its own

argument. So the lemon carries the season,
the moment, shows back itself and not

my own question, not my own deep inhale
and high-pinned thinking, *what is this,*

this emitting. For a time, it is good to be
alone, to not have to share the new fruit

or particular number when thoughts blur,
eyes set on the basket again. Here the girl

reaches sweetness, acidity – hand weighing
one thing only – and takes it in: matte, finite.

Above France

On the streets of Paris, lovers speak of science.
The libraries fill with models in fingerprinted glass.
Nightless prisoners fathom their lifts over walls.

In Annonay, they're filling the balloon with gas
and roping off the crowds. Fields of silk pucker
with buttons in a teacup shade of blue. It billows

as it swells full in the square, engulfs the rustle
of ladies' sleeves, the heat of red cheeks, thoughts
of previous experiments with apparatus. The king

waits for news of the Montgolfier pair. The brothers
choose a geometrician who lusts for maps to come
with them. He poses his instruments. The bag of silk

dimples with light rain. But it lifts. The heated air
fills out its fastened cap. Women finger crosses
around their necks, twist the chains amidst applause.

In the basket, an air soon fills the drawings –
the summit of Montmartre below. Sevres passes
the bounds of the page. St. Cloud, Issy, Ivry offer

their roofs and oldest treetops to the flat white map,
their blinking boulevards dotted with flowered hats.
Sandbags drop to the fields, new coordinates quickly

passed. Then water and rations for extra height,
blankets, parachutes. The views continue onto new
pages, each finished one dropped at the feet of

the pilots, crisp edges catching towns as they roll
closed in spirals on the floor. A careful navigation
follows around the cathedrals, the gorgeous arrows

of their spires. The Academy pauses to squint
from fogged windows at the moonish invention
floating by, dilating in its descent, full of ropes.

Vanishing Point, 1425

There is a way to show this after all.
Brunelleschi, unsure what to do next,
stands in the portal of the open Duomo
staring across the piazza. It's early morning,
and the sun is granting silver leaf to every edge

it finds. In one hand hangs his painting, made
for the experiment, lentil-sized hole center.
The other fist guards a lead-backed
looking glass. It flashes as it fills,
repeats the distance it meets.

The square's begun to fill
with spectators. Constant motions
cloud the view, thus he adjusts the pair
again – front of painting to front of glass –
and peers between the profiles at what results:

quick study of the Baptistry, columns and beams
on a grid. The grid, different: picture measure
with a sense of direction. The scene
pulled forward by something
too far away to name.

The artisan postulates
an advantage to maps: the mirror
informs a distant place, a building in its
sacral skins, and beyond, the deep lean of what
makes us seem so tall – that glint where lines begin

to combine. Out where the world exacts and finishes,
level with the resting eye, the hinge of symmetry
hints – bright point, a continuous departure
one cannot help but watch, addressed
by processions of arches,

humming and wide-eyed in
their regard, their spaces lidless,
granted by their frames, leading silence
gradually into the distance, gesturing to its
place. And every street suggests such sight –

the horizon eases it like a rip, taut surface
instructing geometry's spill. Reticulation:
a notion as easy as pews that bow
to its principles. The center
vanishes, too minute

for division, genesis of
toward. Henceforth, nothing
without relation. Neighbors' heads
align before mass, and behind, the world
recedes. Women carry baskets across coordinates,

warm eggs for another place. Before his face, paint
tosses the house of God into glass. In the mirror,
distance sings to position, lines recognize
their derivation. The door, knocked
ajar, returns a blinking eye.

To Emily

December skies erase us in part,
erased as they are, oceans in all

directions, oceans of glue washed
from glue & the milky way like part

of what's been erased. Planets & smears
over the neighbors', what drifts

in the black – stars & stars &
we have reason: to believe something

of infinity but know night ends: again,
love is mostly motionless,

nothing is replaceable. In what
diamond of the frigid quilt does fire

relight? What shoots across:
what smears. We circle the circling

world in dirt, ground lifting with
the boot: adding the weight of fallen

blue. How can we not be moved
completely: left half on this

turned earth. What is chalk: what
comes back: what black part wants

the truth. What fire starts itself.
Come morning someone traces our steps

& notes: we turned to look north,
paused to sink in one place & melt

the cold a moment with breath out
of bone: to connect what is

to what has not been: points pointed
to on wide open skin.

Night in Winter

Suggest: that the candle is not the light itself, but
the enduring, the space of the darkness around,

no matter the moving flame, no matter the spill
that hardens again, unmade. In the watching of

the flame, suggest: that what has been forgotten
was never really lived. Ask: *was it.* If the candle

forgets itself as it spills over, does it ever exist
again? Follow: does it grieve? Is there room

in the letting for a loss that gets felt? Nothing
stops the burning except the breath. Nothing

stops the dreaming except the sharp bell. Talk:
with the candle, can you talk with the candle

without talking with everything? With something
that outlasts your own letting and lets that too?

Choose: what we get to choose, what we feel,
what we make in the growing dark, a healing.

Susurrus

Some things are true & diffuse:
white in the sea, in the thrashing:

in the horizon opening over
the wind we squint against &

knuckles aching. The same white
sea the whites of our eyes: snow

follows I don't: want to believe
there's nothing left now to open.

I want to bare my throat: the most
personal of the personal: things

we watch for the end: or a means
some invisibility: this is how to

make a line toward something.
Come from it every moment:

again: winter unsaid winter
unending. What risk is there

in quiet space: the white I
need it. I open an envelope.

A friend illustrates five ways.
The figures wine on white paper.

I put it on my wall. Light flashes
back out: we'll wake in the crack

between never and now: hum in
bone: hold so things will come.

No one can explain the dawn:
the air paused & time elapsing.

What winter isn't open: always:
what isn't open that is: always

I breathe the air outside my chest
& whirl & fill & the day quiets

a quiet space sometimes: you
can only whisper to yourself

Infinitesimal

How many words: can we use
for snow or anything we wait for:

for anything we walk through
snow for: leave the window open

to cold for: how many ways
can we touch without leaving: a trace

or fall for what can't be touched
as tongue & snow: can never meet

can never gather all the points:
all that falls onto eyes that close

the many numbering: a pulse
a clock a sky for lost time: I want

to grab it sometimes & make
a fair space: there are places above

us: between salted ice &
a match strike: can you be in your

feet on the ground: let stars
light themselves & drifts line up

one by one: a place cold
enough to keep an edge just: say

what you'll say: I'll say it back:
think only of that & the metal smell

coming a basin: a heaven on
the wind that heralds it & divides us

in two: the snow the heart
a feathered thing & all the falling

things: wisps of crystal & mineral
ozone & a chimney: someone burning

something sweet: what isn't left
to fall until it's infinitesimal: bright

against the window: against
the night: & down to open ground

The Sands

Millicent air trails
snap up from the bed, and the plains

of sine shifting give limit
its shine. I touch my cloud-want

to the surface in
washing, leave my softness in scrub

of bright prism grain.
There's no place to float to, & no

tunnel will stay. Scissors
of light score the circling and return,

the bottom its vacuum,
my outer a chamber, a ring for some

tunneling star.
The tideline is a constant writing.

The most scattered
and felt of the efforts. What letter

can attach to a moving
line. What can you send off into hiss

and sketch. What
does it start with; where does it go

from there. An aspect
has no bounds, a facet no empty point.

Blue and grey rearrange,
pull beneath at our next fluid hour.

Verjuice

This vineyard in winter: fruit formed & brown,
baring the branch as it bares its last. Give me

the end & make it last while it can: through
the night that repeats: it takes so many

to reach what is: rendering the field complete.
We are complete in ending whether

we conclude or not: the finish gives itself
to brown & rain settling. Which of us

really begin inside: in the cupboard I've
got a bottle of verjuice I don't know

what to do with. There is too much light
to see some questions by. At the end

of the walk, the bottom of the vineyard,
a line traces a line in dark: dark

enough to call out all our empty answers:
lines sisters & wishes, twin firsts

Ice Plant

All the transparence of the old
world: grown green & zeroed by saline

so glowing: for winter we are
common as breath & tough as air lost

in space: felt at edge as edge: so
filled we cannot: but become the frost

become the lines we become: at
the coast succulent: the bluff on an empty

day: a day a day spread: so spread
there is nothing beyond but more line &

the air to feel it: mass the same
as space: the same as freezing as zero as red

tips sparkling: too bright a belief
holds the ground and watches dispassionate

as we show: & take the cold spread
in cold sand: we are neon when we come

January

The last persimmon: a moon
a clear interference. A thing pressing

presses: the idea of a door
before the one who notices: moons,

branches. Gods of doors and
gates. Wind blurs: word. Braids dust.

Moons wait in all the waters
of the world. Numerous and definite:

I put my heart out to:
the light. It reads: itself not horizon.

Moon shining in still pool: eyes
casting: another center. What: you love

you cannot cup, lift out.
What you love must: be only what

you love: knowing what
goes unstirred: in the wind around.

Photograph: Lauren Cohn-Frankel

Rae Gouirand's poems have appeared in *American Poetry Review, Boston Review, Columbia, The Kenyon Review: KROnline, Seneca Review, Bateau, jubilat,* two recent volumes of the *Best New Poets* series, and on *Verse Daily.* The winner of the Avery Jules Hopwood Award, the Meijer Fellowship, fellowships from the Vermont Studio Center and the Santa Fe Art Institute, and an award from the Dorothy Sargent Rosenberg Foundation for outstanding work by emerging poets, she lives in Davis, California and serves as Writer-in-Residence for the Cache Creek Conservancy.